To Jeanet

GW01418202

RADIANT FRIENDS 1995-2002

With kind regards

*Tribute compilation of the further paranormal
case-histories and psychic contributions*

of

Kevin McGrath

Psychic, Medium, Healer And Exorcist

DAVID JONES

KEVIN Oct 2012

First published in Great Britain 2002 by
Krystina Bradley, Beau Centre,
Altrincham, Cheshire,
WA14 1HY

Copyright © David Jones 2002

The right of David Jones to be identified as the Author
of the Work has been asserted by him
in accordance with the
Copyright, Designs and Patents Act 1988.

ISBN 0-9531712-2-1

Printed and Typeset in Great Britain
by Bollington Printshop
The Old Stables, Queen Street, Bollington,
Macclesfield, Cheshire SK10 5PS

INTRODUCTION

Following the very successful publication in 1997 of Kevin McGrath's book – "Radiant Friends Beside Me", there has been a continual public demand for him to write a follow-up book.

Owing to family and ongoing commitments, he has been unable to satisfy the many readers' wishes for him to accomplish the task, although he has been deeply touched by the strong appreciation of his psychic services.

Therefore, as a long time admirer of Kevin's unique and abundant spiritual gifts, I have taken a personal pleasure in writing this book, which is a mind-boggling and riveting collection of various case histories, including soul rescues, exorcisms, mediumistic accounts, psychic question and answer contributions and startling spiritual healing cures.

DAVID JONES

"A fascinating compilation of incredible paranormal case histories and the inspirational psychic contributions of Kevin McGrath, a truly special, multi-gifted psychic of the modern era".

ARTHUR HOFFMAN
Psychic and Healer
(With divine help from above)

RADIANT FRIENDS

1995 - 2002

DAVID JONES

Krystina Bradley

ACKNOWLEDGEMENTS

My gratitude is extended to Kevin McGrath's dear wife, Janet for all her tremendous help with the compilation of published material and final completion of this book.

Many thanks also to the Warrington Guardian, Bridge Street, Warrington, Cheshire and The Psychic News, Stansted Hall, Stansted, Essex, for their permission in allowing published articles and letters to be replicated from their newspapers.

Special thanks also to all the kind souls who have unselfishly shared their psychic experiences through the written articles and letters printed in this book.

DEDICATION

A most special dedication to Kevin's Dear Mum, who passed to the higher side 2nd March 2001.

C O N T E N T S

CHAPTER ONE

Hauntings

The following eerie articles involve rescues of earthbound souls and the exorcisms of evil spirits.

Case History Number One

FAMILIES SCARED FROM HOMES BY PHANTOMS

CHILD MOLESTED BY UNKEMPT SPIRIT

The Guardian – August 1996

A Warrington couple have been driven out of a council flat by the ghost of an old woman.

Karen Mahoney, who is eight months pregnant, and her partner, Neil Grady, have been found fresh accommodation by the housing department after Karen became frightened by a spooky presence.

Warrington psychic, Kevin McGrath got rid of the ghost in Densham Avenue, but Karen was too afraid to return.

Said Neil "It was Karen's flat, I stayed with her for a few weeks. There was the sound of an old person mumbling, walking along the hall and in the front room and a sort of clicking noise. It had gone on for five months. Karen was frightened and I didn't know what to do. We moved out and went to stay with her parents in Northway and the council was told about the ghost".

Kevin said he visited the flat and found the ghost of an elderly woman. "She was not related to the family, but she knew them. Karen's grandfather also appeared and he was worried about her. I said the appropriate prayers.

Dog

Karen also revealed that Karen's grandfather had appeared with a dog, which was yapping at him, and the dog had been there to identify him.

Kevin did a "soul rescue" which, he said, is to help non-malevolent spirits to move on to a spirit realm where they are supposed to go to.

"I heard the elderly woman's voice" revealed Kevin. "She said she was pleased because the time was right. She also said she had been a widow when she died".

When he went back outside the flat where Karen and her mother were waiting and related the story, Karen told him that her late grandfather used to have a terrier.

Mr. Tom Roberts, Housing Director, confirmed that Karen would be rehoused but not because of the ghost. "This lady felt she had experienced something and our reaction was on social /medical grounds.

Karen is being given a house in Padgate, and Neil will move in with her.

Kevin also revealed that he had also exorcised a ghost, which appeared to have molested a four-year-old girl in Warrington. The mother, who would not be named, contacted Kevin after a series of incidents, culminating in the assault. She heard her child screaming, rushed to her, and found her pyjamas had been pulled down.

Her body was red and she was complaining of pains in her tummy.

The incident came at the end of a week of problems, including glass being shattered, an older child's bedroom being wrecked and the mother feeling she was being blindfolded, and suffocated.

After the incident with the child, the family went to stay with friends. The mother then contacted Kevin.

Kevin said the ghost was a most unpleasant individual, unkempt and smelly, a man in his forties. "He wanted to fight me and wanted to stay. He didn't want me to move him. I carried out an exorcism and gave the house a full blessing. I saw him shrinking away. It was a very evil spirit. I rang the mother two weeks later and she said everything was OK.

Case History Number Two

PHANTOM IN PINSTRIPES
GRABBED WOMAN'S FOOT

The Guardian – April 1997

A Warrington woman "nearly had a heart attack" when the ghost of a man in a pin-striped suit appeared in her bedroom, and grasped her foot, while she was in bed.

Mrs. Rae Johnson, who lives in the town centre, said the man "followed" her around the house, appearing and disappearing, day and night, for two weeks.

"He petrified me", said Rae. "I could not sleep. I was sitting up all night with the lights on. He wore a brown suit and a gold watch chain and had grey hair and quite a kind, gentle face. I asked him what he wanted and what he was doing there".

"I knew he was a ghost, because he was not solid. Sometimes he was behind me. Sometimes he was walking about the rooms. He was all over the house. When he was in the bedroom, he pushed my foot down into the bed.

Finally, Rae rang Warrington psychic, Kevin McGrath, whose work she had read about in the GUARDIAN.

Rae continued: "He came around the following day. He could tell over the phone that I was very distraught. As soon as he came in, he knew that the man was upstairs. He asked if I had any holy water.

"I had some holy water which a friend had brought from Ireland. Kevin blessed all the rooms downstairs and said prayers. Then we went upstairs, and Kevin saw him. However, I could not see him, although I felt that he was there.

"Kevin asked him to go. He told him not to be afraid and that his loved ones were waiting. He told the man that he would guide him.

ENERGY

"I just had my eyes shut. When Kevin had finished, I felt as if every bit of energy had drained from me."

Rae then described how she felt herself being knocked off balance.

She said: "Something went right through me. Kevin put his hand on my head and said another prayer. The man disappeared and strangely, the whole house felt different. It felt clear".

Kevin told the GUARDIAN that he knew the incident was going to happen before Rae rang him. He has been removing ghosts from buildings in Warrington for more than 20 years and is a well-known psychic.

He said one of his "spirit guides" had told him he had some serious work to do, and that he would help him.

Kevin believes that the "ghost" was that of a man from the 1930s, who worked in finance. He had no connection with Rae.

He said: "My guide gave me the name of Browning. I did an exorcism but he was reluctant to move to the higher side. When he went, the Christ force was so great, it threw Rae off her feet".

Case History Number Three

PSYCHIC CALLED IN AFTER "HAUNTING"

FRIGHTENED MUM TELLS OF GHOSTLY APPARITION AND SPECTRAL FOOTSTEPS

The Guardian – July 1998

Things that go bump in the night made life a misery for Tracy Bowler and her family.

After putting up with months of ghostly disturbances, Tracy discovered that she had no less than three unwelcome 'guests' in her house.

The trouble started soon after Tracy and her three children moved into their home in Orford, last August.

Daughter Rachel, 13, saw a dark-haired man in her bedroom. Also Thomas, eight, was awakened by something going into his bedroom, even though there was nobody there. There were sounds of people clattering upstairs, closing doors and banging on the landing. Relatives who came to stay were as alarmed as the family.

Tracy said: "We tried to put it out of our heads, but we couldn't.

"It really got to me. People think you are daft when you talk about it. You would have to live here to understand it."

She asked a Roman Catholic priest to come in to try to solve the problem and the house went quiet, but only for a short time.

The noises started again and one night, Tracy was kept awake all night after a downstairs door continually kept banging and the sound of someone running up and downstairs was heard.

Finally, a friend put Tracy in touch with Warrington Psychic, Kevin McGrath, who said he had found the spirits of a man who had committed suicide in the house about 15 years ago, a little blonde haired girl of around nine, and an elderly grandfather figure, whom Kevin believed was Tracy's grandfather.

Said Tracy: "Kevin came to the house. He said there are people there from my own family as well as the man who was annoying us.

"One was a little girl called Sarah Ann. It didn't know anyone of this name, but when I asked my grandmother if there was anyone she could remember, she said her twin sister, who died at the age of nine months was called Sarah Ann.

UNWELCOME

"Kevin got rid of all of them and everything has been quiet since. It's brilliant! I want people to know about it".

Kevin said that his "spirit guides" had told him who the unwelcome strangers were.

He said: "The man who committed suicide was causing distress to Tracy's family. I carried out a "soul rescue". I said some prayers. They were powerful, comforting and full of love, and he was guided on to the Higher side, through a channel of light".

"The elderly man was being protective to Tracy and her family".

Case History Number Four

GHOSTLY TALE OF PERCY AND THE POACHER

Flying glasses and psychic energy in haunted pub

The Guardian – February 1999

Customers at a Croft pub are getting more than they bargain for when they ask for spirits. The pub doesn't just stock the alcoholic variety!

Despite well-known psychic Kevin McGrath exorcising two ghosts, a few strange happenings have taken place. Glasses have fallen over and an 1851 farthing was found in a disused room.

Landlady June Clarke said: "Kevin says that after the ghosts have gone, a residue of energy is left. This will eventually go, but in the meantime things keep happening."

Kevin agreed: "The reason the glasses moved was due to one of the bar staff giving off psychic energy. This combusted with the residual energy which was left because the building was haunted for so long. It will go as time goes on."

June says there have been spooky happenings at the pub for many years. "The draymen have always said there was something in the cellar," she said. "The burglar alarm was going off every hour, the dog was barking like mad at nothing and there were ice cold areas in the pub."

"When a sash window opened and slammed closed of its own accord, June decided the time had come to seek help. "I had read about Kevin McGrath in the GUARDIAN", she said. "He says we had two ghosts, one upstairs and one downstairs. Living upstairs was a poacher called Stanley Cummings who died 150 years ago. He didn't know he was dead and was going through the motions of working. Kevin said that the downstairs ghost was a more recent death and called him Percy. He pointed to the place where he sat and said that he had done lots of walking along the carpet".

Case History Number Five

CALLING TIME ON PUB'S UNWANTED GUESTS

The Guardian – March 1999

If you visit a pub you expect there to be a wide variety of spirits on offer but what happens when the spirits aren't of the alcoholic variety and he pub's regulars report strange goings on?

GUARDIAN reporter Suzanne Elsworth attended an exorcism at a haunted hostelry to try to find the truth behind the spooky tales.

I have always been fascinated by the paranormal, so when Warrington psychic Kevin McGrath invited me to watch an exorcism of the Raven Inn in Glazebury I just couldn't refuse.

The pub's licensees, Janet and Steve Allen moved there six month's ago and, despite hearing about haunting tales from customers, they didn't notice anything out of the ordinary – until one night in January when they were woken by a crash, as trays of cutlery fell to the floor. They thought nothing of it and placed the trays in a neat row behind the bar where they could not overbalance.

But the next morning the cutlery was again scattered across the floor. Even the unflappable Janet felt uneasy, as no-one had been in the room but herself. When Kevin read about the spooky happenings in the GUARDIAN he immediately came to the couple's aid. Janet and Steve admit that they were sceptical about the exorcism, but agreed to go through with it after Kevin explained that other, more psychically sensitive people may suffer.

Kevin told me that there were the spirits of a woman and man in the pub and their presence was especially strong near the kitchen area. The pair, though totally unrelated, both dated back to the Georgian era. He was a carpenter and also worked with coaches, while she cooked at the inn.

"The woman had died from pneumonia, but she clung to the pub when she was asked to move on." said Kevin.

"She was most insistent that she did not want people in there. There was no evil force evident, but she didn't take kindly to people taking over her duties."

After sprinkling liberal amounts of holy water and blessing the building, Kevin was finally satisfied that the restless and troublesome spirits had finally moved on, but he did say that the pub would probably never be free of ghosts. "There will always be some atmosphere here because the pub absorbs it", he added.

I had no idea what to expect when I agreed to attend an exorcism. Apart from a couple of visits to a medium, I had never been in close contact with spirits before.

Would glasses go flying across the room, as in a story I wrote about ghosts in Croft's General Elliot? Or would I wish I'd put my thermals on when the pub suddenly went icy cold?"

Case History Number Six

TRUE ACCOUNT OF A MOST HARROWING PSYCHIC EXPERIENCE

from Christina Kroft of Little Bollington, Cheshire

Letter to the National Press – November 1999

I recently had the most awful experience and I hope you will find this account of its resolution of interest to your readers.

I am a reasonably successful businesswoman and my husband and I are privileged to live in an old house in the country. For many years this has been a very peaceful residence. However, three months ago, for no reason apparent to us, we started to live out a complete nightmare.

We were continually woken during the night with the sound of doors being slammed throughout the house. I began to see faces of men and women appearing on the bedroom walls and all sorts of coloured lights started showering us as we lay in bed.

The final straw came when the wardrobe doors were being banged very loudly in the spare room throughout the night. To say that I became frightened is a gross understatement. Nevertheless, I was also annoyed and went to investigate.

As I crossed the landing, I was almost overpowered by the most disgusting of smells. Bottles that had been placed on the high timber dresser were being thrown at me by some invisible force.

A crucifix that was fixed on the wall was hurled at my feet. Then, to my complete horror, a hideous and dark figure, resembling a gargoyle, materialised at my side and was pushing itself against my body in brutal and most vile manner.

In complete terror, I ran back to our bedroom, told my husband what had taken place and could think of nothing else to do but pray for help.

The next day, I contacted certain spiritual organisations in London and was advised to consult the Warrington-based psychic, medium and exorcist Kevin McGrath. It transpires that Kevin is well-known for his mediumship, healing, psychic and soul rescue work.

I was desperate so I contacted Kevin straight away and, after I had explained my problem, he agreed to deal with this "haunting" as soon as possible.

Two days later, Kevin arrived at our house and quickly located the entity which he said was of a very evil disposition. He also said it had been attracted to the psychic energy that I was giving out as I was latently developing psychically myself.

As Kevin commenced the exorcism, a tremendous gust of air swept throughout the house accompanied by an awful and obnoxious smell and it seemed that every ornament in the house was rattling at the same time and my dog began to continuously howl.

A full blessing was then carried out and, almost immediately, a wonderful sense of peace returned and my dog stopped howling.

When Kevin left, he assured me that the entity was now finally removed and, to my pleasant surprise, would not take a penny for his services. His reward, he said, was simply to carry out God's work.

Needless to say my husband and I are so grateful to Kevin McGrath for bringing this awful situation to an end and to those who kindly referred me to him.

CHAPTER TWO

Contact Spiritual Healing Experiences

The undermentioned healing episodes confirm the awesome power, that has been conveyed by Kevin McGrath through his spirit guides, to effect the cures as reported.

Letter No 1 to Psychic News – December 1996

PAIN DISAPPEARS
AFTER SPIRITUAL HEALING

I am writing to you further to a telephone conversation we had in late September regarding Mr. Kevin McGrath.

During the past fifteen years I have suffered from what I thought was arthritis in both knees, which caused severe pain and it also limited my movements.

On various visits to my doctor, I was told that it was probably a trapped nerve in my back that would eventually ease in time. Painkillers only provided minimal relief and so I lived with the discomfort and accepted it as part of life.

Towards the latter part of this summer the pain was becoming more and more of a hindrance. At this time, I was given Kevin's telephone number by a friend. I contacted Kevin and discussed my symptoms over the telephone. I told him all about the pain in my knees and legs.

Kevin instantly diagnosed the problem did not lie in my legs but was coming from my back. I made an appointment for a few days later to pay him a visit at his home. The first thing he did was to place his hands on my back. He confirmed his diagnosis made over the telephone was correct and the pain stemmed from three slipped discs. Kevin performed healing treatment, which gave me instant relief. I was asked to return a week later. He explained that the treatment would possibly take several weeks.

On the second visit, just one week later Kevin examined my back. He placed his hands on my back again and I felt instant heat from his hands. Kevin informed me that the process of healing had been so rapid that I would not have to make any further appointments and that my problem had been resolved in just two visits.

Since then, I have been virtually pain free and have been able to do things that I had previously thought would be too painful to attempt.

Brian Ashton, Cheshire

Letter No 2 to Psychic News – February 1997

FIRST AID FROM KEVIN McGRATH

Brian Hannis, Secretary of the North Western Foundation for Spiritual Truth in Cheshire, expressed his wholehearted thanks and that of other group members to Kevin McGrath, the medium and healer for a recent evening of psychic and spiritual enlightenment, which was, as Brian says, "At it's very best, despite knowing that he was also carrying a serious family health concern."

Brian continues, "The continuous power conveyed from the higher side during the evening via Kevin's spirit guides was further confirmed by two remarkable cases of spiritual healing; both involving serious back conditions.

As Kevin was about to leave, one of our members, William Hirst, unexpectedly slipped, and suffered a slipped spinal disc and was clearly in great discomfort and unable to move. His sister voiced her intention to telephone his Specialist for medical help.

Kevin promptly stepped forward and stroked his back for a few minutes. Amazingly, William straightened up fully recovered and free of pain, much to his relief and disbelief!

The second case was following a chance remark from myself to Kevin that my neighbour, Ms. Val Gibson had been ordered to take complete bed rest by her GP for a six week period because of her severe back pain and sciatica following a recent operation.

Kevin again insisted on visiting the house and attending to her condition.

Incredibly, again, within a few minutes of Kevin applying spiritual healing, Val's pain had been totally removed with full mobility restored".

Brian concludes, "I and other members present that night learned much spiritual truth from the experience.

May other needy souls cross the path of this uniquely gifted man."

Letter No 3 to Psychic News – January 1998

HELP THROUGH KINDNESS

In August 1997 I was rushed to hospital with suspected meningitis.

At the age of 24 with no previous health problems, I had my whole life ahead of me. My friends and family thought this was soon to be taken away.

My parents tell me that I was delirious for the first few days and within three weeks in hospital my condition had deteriorated rapidly and I lost five stones.

The results of tests were not good. The platelets in my blood were low. An X-ray had shown that gross abnormalities had developed on my liver. My heart was weak and my blood pressure was high.

After three weeks the blood transfusion, the antibiotics, the saline drip and the special case were all in vain. I was discharged from hospital with a lack of diagnosis from the very best specialists.

However, it must be said that all the staff involved in my care were exceptional.

On discharge, I visited Kevin McGrath. I was introduced to Kevin through my fiancée who had persuaded me to see him after hearing about his work with the sick.

I was reluctant. Through ignorance I was unaware of this type of healing although through her persistence I arranged a visit.

I was very weak and couldn't walk. Kevin helped me into his living room and sat me down. Through Kevin, was given a total diagnosis from the higher side. I was told I had a rare form of meningitis.

Kevin recommended vitamins and a special diet in order to build up my immune system otherwise I would not have had the strength to fight the illness. My body was under attack.

Through a healing session I was given a boost of energy to help me in my steps to recovery. Fifteen months later, I am recovered. I feel strong, energetic and full of life. Kevin has kept in touch with advice, help, support, thoughts, distance healing and good wishes.

Kevin suffers a great deal in helping others. He is selfless and takes nothing in return. His kind-heartedness has given me back my life.

Those who question why people help others should be questioned themselves. Why do some not accept that there are people in the world who help others as a part of human kindness.

Those who do know Kevin will, I am sure, have maintained a strong and lasting friendship with him.

Scott Rylance, Warrington, Cheshire

Letter No 4 to Psychic News – March 1998

I was lucky enough to receive Kevin McGrath's expert spiritual healing which cured a very painful and serious neck condition when all painkillers and medical treatment had failed.

My sister was also fortunate for him to clear a very powerful and disturbing haunting problem with his psychic expertise at her home in Stockport. In both cases, Kevin would not accept payment.

For many years he has regularly been consulted by national TV and radio networks to offer his expert advice on paranormal matters. It is a fact that he is rightly regarded as a leading psychic and healer throughout the UK and overseas.

His reputation is such that he has in the past lectured and demonstrated his psychic skills at the University of Manchester to top medical doctors and scientific researchers, receiving glowing praise for his expertise from his audience.

In my opinion, considering his outstanding credentials in the psychic and clairvoyant field, we the readers have been most fortunate for him to have volunteered to help us through his unique, God-given gifts.

Mrs. K Barnes, Warrington, Cheshire

Letter No 5 to Psychic News – March 1999

PAIN LEFT

Being a newcomer to the Spiritualist movement, I visited Kevin McGrath in September 1999 to receive healing for a long-standing and very painful, serious shoulder condition, which I had suffered with for many years.

I was a trifle apprehensive when I visited Kevin and fully expected a fairly long treatment session. My problem had caused me much depression because it had failed to respond to all conventional medical treatments and as a health care professional, this added to my disillusionment. I must admit I was surprised that during my appointment with Kevin, his healing application lasted just two minutes, in which he cured my condition and for good measure provided an exact diagnosis of my long-standing problem.

To the present day I am pleased to report that I am still pain-free and fully fit. I just wish to thank Kevin McGrath through Psychic News pages for his marvellous gift, which enabled me to resume my career. He is indeed a prize asset to our growing Spiritualist movement.

P Filson, Sutton-in-Craven

Letter No 6 to Psychic News – October 2000

EXPRESSING THANKS THROUGH PSYCHIC NEWS

The recent letters in reader's forum discussing the different merits of spiritual healing have been most interesting, especially so in the light of my own deeply satisfying psychic experience that I too wish to share (if you would be kind enough to print it).

I have known for a long time of Kevin McGrath's reputation as a psychic and medium and of the great success he has widely achieved through absent healing and psychic surgery. However, in a simple and straightforward manner, Kevin has positively transformed my life and more importantly, my husband, had been treated in 1999 for cancer with strong chemotherapy and radiotherapy but was still unwell, his life force being at a low ebb. I myself depressed and in pain from constant headaches was proving insufferable to live with and also having a young child to care for was making matters worse. With nothing to lose, I wrote to Kevin for help.

I received a reply with an appointment promptly arranged. He spent an hour with me during my visit without an exorbitant fee being demanded (unlike another case that was recently highlighted in PN). A quiet kindness and assurance was also felt throughout. The power of spirit I experienced by is presence alone, completely uplifted me. As Stephen was unable to travel, Kevin placed him on his ongoing list for prayer. Without doubt, a dramatic upward change in our health has since materialised and now a very clear light has emerged at the end of our long personal tunnel.

With a wish to express our gratitude through PN, Kevin, words seem insufficient, but please accept a massive thank you from both of us.

J Chester, Cheshire

Letter No 7 to Psychic News – November 2001

OPPORTUNITY TO THANK A HEALER

May you afford me the opportunity to express my deep gratitude to healer and medium Kevin McGrath, by way of the Psychic News?

Following a lengthy period of pain and inactivity, being unable to walk properly and undergoing a range of unsuccessful treatments, amazingly, I can now walk freely, without pain, through Kevin's gift of healing.

His quiet and caring manner also lifted my apprehension and helped me enormously.

G Screeton, Cheshire

CHAPTER THREE

Mediumship Accounts

*Clear evidence of natural clairaudience and
clairsentience, demonstrated by Kevin McGrath
is strongly verified by the written accounts of persons,
who have received strikingly accurate information
channelled through him by his Spirit Guides.
This section includes the written account of an
interview between Kevin and a renowned writer
and concerns soul rescue and exorcism.*

Letter to **Psychic** *News – February* **1997**

HEALER AND MEDIUM
KEVIN McGRATH THANKED

A wonderful medium and healer called Kevin McGrath helped me to live and come to terms with things that happened to me.

Kevin gave me absolute evidence of survival of spirit from physical death.

My first spiritual experience began with Kevin in 1991. My brother Kishore was seriously ill with heart problems and doctors had given up hope. Kevin sent absent healing to aid my brother through an operation. The doctors said he would not survive it but Kevin assured me that his guides had informed him that they would attend to him and he would come home. To the doctor's astonishment Kishore was able to be discharged from hospital. Sadly, some years later his heart finally gave out.

Kevin's mediumship was responsible for bringing my dear mother's presence to my side. He told me my mother loved yellow/red roses and was always in the kitchen. When my mother was alive she had roses in every room in the house and she was the best cook in the family, always trying out new recipes. She also told Kevin what her maiden name was which left me flabbergasted. He also told me about her sister who died a long time ago. I disputed this fact with Kevin as I was not aware of it but he was right as my family informed me later.

Kevin also helped my niece, who was born with a hole in her heart. Here, again doctors held no hope of her recovering from an emergency operation at only six weeks old but through Kevin's healing gift, she pulled through and is now a lively 5 year old.

Going back to my brother Kishore, who passed from that heart condition, he contacted Kevin from the spirit world, because we were grieving badly for him. Although I am a Hindu, Kevin McGrath has proved beyond doubt that we are all God's children. May this message help other readers.

One of the best messages I received was about a blue crystal that belonged to Kishore when he was alive and where to locate it. Many times Kevin described my brother in spirit wearing a silk green and red scarf on is head and decorated with jewels and looking very happy and healthy.

To me this symbolically signifies our Goddess who is always depicted dressed in such attractive saris. Kevin would never have known about this.

Only a week ago Kevin phoned me to tell me Kishore, my brother told him to say "Jai Ambe" to my father who is 86 years old and told him to look after his stomach. Over the last few weeks my father has been unwell and had problems with his stomach and "Jai Ambe" is the name of our Goddess. When Kevin told me this message it warmed the hearts of the family very greatly and provided further amazement.

I hope this helps other people to know that we live on, and to thank Kevin McGrath for bringing us such help.

Mina Rajdev, London

Letter to Psychic News – January 1998

WHEN MEDIUMSHIP IS A LIFE-SAVER

Although being a Psychic News reader of many years I have never written to the paper. However, on this occasion I felt I had to share my most rewarding spiritual experience regarding the incredible mediumship of Kevin McGrath.

Dr. Bessie Howarth, a physician and surgeon of Paignton, Devon, and a lifelong friend had been Kevin's patient for some time before she passed over in her eighties through natural causes.

Through Dr. Howarth's early recommendation, my husband Brian and myself fell under his "healing wing". Our various complaints have always been successfully treated.

Fortunately for us, during one recent visit, he donned his "medium's" cap. My husband had been feeling unwell with no obvious cause. Kevin acting immediately on a firm message from one of his guides, "Dr. Wan Chan" insisted that Brian should obtain a rapid referral from his GP to the local hospital, as he was suffering from a very serious blood disorder, also adding that the application of spiritual healing would not be sufficient as life saving treatment was immediately required.

Acting on Kevin's advice we visited our GP that evening. Following examination, the doctor prescribed tranquillisers, stating that my husband should soon be OK. However, the next day, he still felt off colour.

We again visited Kevin who, within minutes, almost pushed us to the hospital, stating that no time could be spared. Fortunately, Brian was admitted following my protestations.

Needless to say, after exhaustive tests by the Consultant my husband underwent intensive treatment, receiving countless blood transfusions over a period of ten days which indeed saved his life.

Thanks to Kevin McGrath and his wonderful guide, my dear husband is now fully recovered and stronger than ever. Kevin was immensely happy after I informed him of Brian's progress.

His closing remarks were quite profound, "Alice, It was not God's wish for Brian to go over, an instrument was chosen which happened to be me, to ensure that he didn't."

Nonetheless, we owe him our heartfelt gratitude. Without his pinpoint clairvoyance my husband would not be alive today.

Alice Timpson, Lancashire

Letter to Psychic News – July 1998

TELEPHONE EVIDENCE
FROM HEALER KEVIN

I became interested in Spiritualism some twenty-two years ago during a very distressing time in my life. I know now, in hindsight, that I was gently guided towards a new way of thinking and believing in order to be able to cope with the upheavals that I faced in later years.

I now live in Cyprus but I continue to receive my weekly copy of Psychic News. I cannot go without it. Furthermore, I buy a very great number of books from the mail order department where David Bardwell is ever so helpful in despatching them speedily.

However, the purpose of this letter is to praise and express my gratitude for psychic, medium and healer, Kevin McGrath. I have never met him in person nor have I spoken to him before. I communicated with Kevin by telephone having received his number from the Psychic News.

I was given over the telephone, and I labour the point, over the telephone, irrefutable evidence, so startling, that I went cold in my stomach, from the shock. Among other information given, my father came through whom Kevin described accurately, and advised me that I should read the Silver Birch series of books, as in them I shall find all the answers that I seek.

What Kevin McGrath did not know, and there was no way of him knowing, is the fact that I have by my bedside table six books of Silver Birch teachings, together with the beloved Guide's photograph in postcard form. All of them having been purchased in October 1996. Somehow, I never got round to reading them, deferring that for a later date.

I had doubts and I had questions. I prayed for guidance and the way was shown to me through Kevin. The hand of God is forever guiding us, if only we ask.

I wish for others to be helped by Kevin, as I was.

He never asked for money up front. A donation was suggested, the amount to be at my discretion.

Thank you Kevin.

H Demos, Cyprus

Featured in Psychic News Article – February 1999

KEVIN McGRATH ANSWERS
10 QUESTIONS ABOUT SOUL RESCUE

Ernie Sears, a well-known authority on UFO phenomena, healer and Psychic News contributor, recently interviewed Kevin McGrath, the renowned psychic, medium, healer and leading exorcist.

The interview specifically concerned Kevin's exorcism and soul rescue services in line with the needs of those who have undergone unpleasant, unnerving experiences of this type, for those needing help now, and those who may experience similar problems in the future.

Q.	*Why and when did you branch off into this form of spiritual work and who trained you?*

A.	I first commenced exorcism and soul rescue work approximately 15 years ago following very powerful prompting by my premier guide, Brother Paul, a Franciscan Monk. It became clear that I was incarnated with a principal duty to include this important mediumistic work with my other spiritual services. The procedures were given through the instruction of Brother Paul and my other spirit guides.

Q.   *Why are so many souls lodged in an earthbound state and why are some of these evil in nature*

A.   On transition from the earth life all souls still possess free will. But some, for personal reasons, refuse to accompany their guardian spirits on the pathway of light where they would eventually be greeted by family loved ones who have previously passed. Nonetheless, a properly conducted soul rescue operation usually resettles souls who are lost, confused or plain stubborn.

Souls are evil in nature because they were of a similar disposition during their previous earth life. One's persona does not change on transition to the spirit world.

However, the removal of evil or inferior spirits is a different and more difficult task. I sometimes pay a personal price for my efforts as negative forces, fuelled by frustration, seek reprisal by creating great difficulties with my domestic electrical supply, appliances and telephone lines, etc.

Fortunately, the Divine protection provided by the Higher side prevents a direct attack on my auric field which otherwise could be very dangerous to my health.

Q. *It is widely believed that our guardian spirits protect us from such evil entities. If so, why do so many people suffer episodes of malevolent haunting, often with infliction of severe physical harm or emotional and mental distress?*

A. Inferior spirits choosing to remain earthbound know that, should they move through the astral gateway leading to the spirit realms, an unpleasant existence awaits them on one of the lower planes. Others, of a similar disposition, gravitate there as a result of their low vibrations and their karmic responsibilities being increased as a result of their un-Godly lives during their previous incarnation on the Earth plane.

    While possessing divine power, our guardian spirits do not have the strength needed to forcibly remove these spirits to their rightful place in the spirit planes. Therefore, an Earth channel is chosen to eject them through the invocation of the Christ force, via the God-Head, with guides strongly in attendance who are specially assigned to the medium for this vital work.

Q. *Your other spiritual duties must take up much of your time and energy. Considering the concentration required, does exorcism and soul rescue deplete your energies and how many cases on average do you carry out?*

A   I normally carry out approximately 30 exorcisms or soul rescues per year. Fortunately, my mediumistic and spiritual healing duties do not cause me too much fatigue so I usually feel quite sound and alert after the completion of the spirit clearance.

Q.   *Do you undergo any special preparations prior to carrying out an exorcism or soul rescue?*

A.   Yes, I meditate strongly and protect my aura with a special and very effect ancient monk's prayer. A visit to a Church is normal to enable me to immerse myself in the Christ Force and pray to the God Head for the extra power that will be required for the task to be undertaken.

Q.   *I remember some years ago that in one of your articles, you warned about the casual use of Ouija boards. Could you clarify this issue further?*

A.   My view on the dangerous use of the Ouija board has not changed. Over the years, I have encountered various evil and hostile spirit entities which gave considerable resistance and needed strong exorcism. A high percentage had been invited by well meaning but naïve people carelessly using the Ouija board in a home setting.

Communication with the spirit world in this uncontrolled manner can send immediate signals to the discarnate groups of 'riff-raff' congregating within the corridors of the astral plane that are adjacent to our own earth plane. These inferior, troublesome souls can quickly grasp the opportunity to wreak psychic havoc on the unfortunate board users and their contacts.

If, for bona fide reasons, a person seeks contact with souls who have passed on, I recommend they consult with a reputable spiritual medium or attend a service in a Spiritualist National Union Church or Greater World Church. Both offer realistic safeguards for the future mental and physical wellbeing of the seeker.

Q.   *Have you had any failures when you have been consulted to deal with spirit disturbances etc?*

A.   To the present time, apart from alleged spirit hauntings which provided to be features of structural movement or other natural matters, each genuine case I have been involved with has happily been brought to a successful conclusion.

However, some people are natural clairvoyants who will always be aware of spirit and may experience further sightings. Also, the Higher side does arrange carefully controlled return visits of loved ones for them to be close once again to those still living their Earth lives.

Q.   *Should the Spiritualist network offer more special training courses so that suitable, willing mediums can increase their development to carry out this special service?*

A.   It would please me greatly if more teaching was available from mediums experienced in exorcism and soul rescue work, but I do understand that such mediums are usually very busy. A gradual teaching programme undertaken by development circles may be the ideal solution.

Q.   *You included an instruction section in your latest book. Would you be prepared to release it on a general basis for those with Godly intentions?*

A.   I would be pleased to release these procedures to all those wishing to use them constructively.

Q.   *Do you ever see a time when haunting and spirit possession will cease to be a problem in our world?*

A.   Through God's perfect laws, the Universe is forever evolving and the Earth will inevitably be pulled along that evolutionary path. There will come a time when all individual spirits created by God, because of their higher vibrations, will enjoy an existence in the upper spirit realms. The planet Earth will naturally become redundant for its teaching purposes and for the evolution of young souls.

Letter to Psychic News – December 1999

SYNCHRONICITY BY THE BOOK

I read with interest the letter from Mike Barrymore, PN November 13th 1999 regarding the power of books to inspire and uplift people.

After reading the wonderful book "Radiant Friends Beside Me" by medium and healer Kevin McGrath my whole being was quickly rejuvenated. It was a most welcome tonic following an illness. The spirit world also seem to uncannily arrange other forms of timely upliftment and confirmation, especially with the book I have mentioned.

A friend and I recently bumped into Mr. McGrath at a holistic workshop in Manchester. My friend's wife had recently passed over, leaving him quite low. On meeting Kevin McGrath I took the opportunity to express my appreciation of his book. He warmly acknowledged the thanks and then quickly broke off our conversation to convey and amazing message to my friend from his wife in spirit. The details provided were so accurate and personal that the sense of loss that surrounded him was immediately banished.

May I thank Kevin through the Psychic News for his most kind act, as his book would suggest, he truly is a unique instrument for the higher side.

Elaine Kearns, Derbyshire

Letter to Psychic News – December 1999

POETIC PRAISE WRITTEN FOR KEVIN

I write to reinforce the viewpoint of Mike Barrymore (May 22, PN) that well known mediums do indeed take the trouble to serve small churches and groups, contrary to those who have written otherwise.

One of our leading channels, Kevin McGrath, recently honoured his agreement to give an evening of teaching and mediumship at our Poets and Writers quarterly meeting in Altrincham. This commitment was made twelve months earlier.

Kevin's superb address, and faultless clairvoyance, convinced a number of my fellow writers of the spiritual truth of survival. This is particularly heart warming, as they previously doubted even the existence of the spirit world, let alone the broad abilities of a good medium.

We further appreciated Kevin's meeting of his commitment when we realised that he kept the engagement in spite of the serious illness of a close member of his family.

He arrived on time, he was modest, down to earth and not at all egotistical, and we now know that, apart from his well documented and valuable healing works, he also teaches and writes about a diversity of psychic and spiritual matters, including soul rescue and the clearance of entities which sometimes are not of good intentions.

We sympathise with anyone who has been let down by mediums, but would thank and recommend Kevin for his own diligence and commitment to his work, and the warmth but no-fuss manner with which he conducts it.

Thomas Jacobs, Cheshire

CHAPTER FOUR

Distant Spiritual Healing Experiences

*Many souls who had been suffering from a wide range of
health conditions, have undergone incredible healing cures
through distance healing. No physical contact had been made
between themselves and Kevin McGrath. Written healing
requests received have been focused upon by him at fixed times,
with subsequent visits made by his spirit guides to the
patients concerned, resulting in the inexplicable cures
that are mentioned in the following letters.*

Letter No 1 to Psychic News – December 1996

PRAISE FOR KEVIN McGRATH AND HIS HEALING GUIDES

I have received an inestimable amount of help through spiritual healing from Kevin McGrath. Kevin tells me that his guides have interceded on several occasions to improve the condition of my mother who is suffering from cancer. She had a difficult operation early last year and we almost lost her in hospital but as a result of speaking to Kevin she rallied, and even more, she overcame a subsequent fall and crushed vertebrae as a result. Within thirty-six hours she was on her feet again and was able to walk eight kilometres in one go.

I hope this information is useful and will provide an extra avenue of help where sometimes people have given up.

Susan Muir, Manchester

Letter No 2 to Psychic News – January 1997

HEALING OVER THE TELEPHONE

In reference to Kevin McGrath the healer, I would like your readers to know that 5 years ago my doctor decided that I had arthritis in my right leg and that I had to live with it. During the years walking became from bad to worse. I could hardly put my weight on the right leg, the pain was crucifying. Two weeks ago I decided to phone Kevin. After having spoken to Kevin about my troubled leg he advised me to phone back after a week, during which he would ask for healing for me. I phoned Kevin, he told me that he would reduce the pain but could not cure me completely. The following morning I experienced no pain in resting on my leg and could walk properly for the first time in years.

J Brizee, Eire

Letter No 3 to Psychic News – March 1998

PRAISE FOR HEALER KEVIN

Some time last year I wrote to a healer after seeing his name and testimonials advertised.

My husband was very ill at the time and I was desperate to get healing for him. His doctor (a good one) had done all he could for him, so getting help from spirit was my last hope.

I wrote to the healer just mentioned and got a prompt reply telling me of his overheads and requesting a donation before healing could start and a letter and further donations every two weeks! That decided me that I didn't want him.

In my opinion, he isn't a caring person, but one who loves money. He rang me and asked why I hadn't been in touch. I told him we were pensioners with limited income and could not afford donations every two weeks ....end of story!!

Kevin McGrath came to my attention, via Psychic News. So many people have written praising him for the wonderful way they have been helped by him.

I've recently had occasion to ring him regarding the illness of my granddaughter who has "lupus" a very rare disease. He has helped me on three other occasions with success. I wrote to him over the weekend including a donation, which was returned with a very nice letter saying that the donation was not necessary.

My example of two totally different healers.

One worships money, the other to give of his great gift. Talking to him over the telephone, love and caring oozed from him. He isn't a rich man.

Getting rich is not his main concern.

June Graham, Berwickshire

Letter No 3 to Psychic News – September 1998

PSYCHIC SPINAL SURGERY SUCCESS

I want everybody to know that I have had miraculous psychic surgery carried out on what was my twisted spine by Kevin McGrath and his "Radiant Ones" – the spiritual team that work so well together, relieving people's suffering.

Earthly surgeons had pronounced an emphatic "No" to me ever being able to straighten a spine after fifteen years and "they" are still working on parts of my anatomy and they will not stop until I am relieved of all pain.

Please, if you are suffering, like I was and for whatever reason, do contact Kevin and his wonderful spiritual team. I can assure you that you will feel better after talking to him as his healing comes right through the phone! He truly is a marvellous healer.

Please God let him heal for a long time yet.

Name & Address Supplied
Isle of Wight

Letter No 4 to Psychic News – October 1998

HEALER KEVIN McGRATH DOES IT AGAIN

I would be very grateful if you print the following in your letters page.

Some two to three years ago I read in PN, letters from people who had consulted and been healed by medium and healer Kevin McGrath. I thought "how wonderful", cut them out and filed them away in case I might need to address in the future.

In July this year I went to Austria on holiday by coach. On the journey to Dover I was struck by a dreadful pain in my left leg. It was very bad, it lasted for weeks and painkillers did not ease the situation. My doctor made an appointment for me to see an orthopaedic surgeon.

Still awaiting an appointment by the end of July, I was desperate and decided to write to Kevin. Within two days the pain had eased. I realised he must have had my letter. Because of my own commitments I could not get to visit Kevin as he requested but, no problem, "the radiant ones", who can work independently from him, visited me.

I don't see or hear spirit, but Kevin told me approximately what time something would happen and sure enough, during that time the pain went. It was a trapped sciatic nerve.

After, my pack pain, which I had had for about ten years, which I had not mentioned to Kevin, was also cured.

October arrived and I had a new pain in the same leg, very severe but nothing like the sciatic problem. I phoned Kevin straight away and within a few seconds he informed me it was phlebitis. Once again, within a short time, I was cured.

The object of this letter is not just to praise Kevin, "my man of miracles" as I now refer to him, but to urge anyone who needs help to contact him. When asked what his charges were I received an emphatic "no charge".

Mrs Davis, Connah's Quay, Wales

Letter No 6 to Psychic News – December 1998

ANOTHER PSYCHIC
SPINAL SURGERY SUCCESS

Terry Hands, a PN reader from Northampton is over the moon as they say after receiving absent healing from Kevin McGrath.

Terry takes up the story, "In the September 5 issue I read how Kevin McGrath and his "Radiant Ones" had corrected the contributor's twisted spine.

I've needed osteopaths or chiropractors for years but they couldn't help with my recent, excruciating slipped disc and indescribable leg pains.

I only knew of a good friend's intervention when Kevin wrote to offer me help. By the time I got his letter he had already requested absent healing for me.

An MRI scan clearly showed an enormously bulging disc pressing deeply into my sciatic nerve but, six days after this scan was taken, and after Kevin's guides had visited me, a consultant surgeon could not understand how I was standing, let alone able to move freely, stand straight and be without bad pain. My back is now straighter and stronger than it has been for years!

I was doubly blessed by actually seeing one of Kevin's guides – a beautiful experience worth all the pain that I previously had!

I endorse totally the article of September 5th. If you are suffering badly whatever the cause, please contact Kevin straight away

Terry Hands, Northampton

Article featured in The Guardian – January 1999

HAIRDRESSER CURED BY MIRACLE FAITH HEALER

A Warrington hairdresser who was only given a 50-50 chance of survival is crediting the spirit world with her remarkable recovery.

Susan Abbot, of Folly Lane, was gravely ill in Liverpool's Royal Hospital with a burst appendix and peritonitis which was poisoning her blood stream when her mum Alice Whittaker called in a spiritual healer in desperation.

Alice of Great Sankey, a member of the spiritualist church, had read of Kevin McGrath's exploits in a newspaper.

Kevin told Alice that his guides had visited Susan in the hospital and, the next day, doctors apparently noticed an improvement in her condition.

Susan's husband said "The doctors had told us that her chances were less than 50-50 and they were trying to prepare us for the worst".

"Sue's mum called Kevin and he said help would continue. The next day doctors had another look at Susan and told me that they were surprised. They did some tests and they showed a definite improvement".

It will be several months before Susan aged 47 will be recovered to full health but her experience has taken her by surprise.

She said, "It has proved to me what can really happen. Some people laugh and say, "you must be joking". But things do happen and it has to have happened to you. There are things which we don't know about."

Letter No 7 to Psychic News – February 2000

ASKING FOR PRAYERS

Being a spiritualist healer for just over five years I ask for all your healing prayers to go out to these people who have recently been in the daily tabloids, suffering with inoperable cancers and tumours.

Mavis Skeet, Ray Weir, Terry Nixon, Amy Hall, and so many others. I ask all the healers to place them on their healing lists.

I would also like to thank Kevin McGrath who has given me a link with his healing guides and helped one of my patients who suffered with a tumour on the pancreas and cancer running away on the liver. After his scan at the hospital a few weeks ago, the doctors were dumfounded and cannot explain what's going on. He is now clear. Thank you Kevin McGrath and your loving healers.

Keith Rosser, Essex

Letter No 8 to Psychic News – May 1999

HIGHLIGHTING SPIRITUAL HEALING

Having read the letter of Keith Rosser in the issue of February 12th, in which he confirmed that a pancreatic tumour and liver cancer had been cured through a surge of distant spiritual healing via Kevin McGrath's spirit guides, I must admit that it intrigued me why this glorious example of spiritual healing was not "shouted from the rooftops" through the general media, press, etc.

I am sure the medics would have certainly taken their kudos for the remarkable and welcome change in the patient's condition.

As Spiritualists, we must not undersell ourselves; let the glorious truth be known to all whenever possible. The sceptics, scientific and medical must be won over, however difficult and long it will take. This particular powerful example of healing mediumship, if highlighted, can only help towards this end.

Mr B Johnson, Cheshire

Letter No 9 to Psychic News – August 1999

NIGHT HEALING

I suffer from osteo-arthritis in my hips and knees and spondylosis (where the bones fuse together) in my lower back. The arthritis causes stiffness, but the spondylosis gave me real pain. When I got up from a sitting position I couldn't straighten up. I had to wait till the pain and stiffness went before I could walk.

I had read Kevin McGrath's book and thought of writing for help and then I read about the help Terry Hands had received from Kevin in the June 19 issue of Psychic News. That made my mind up and I wrote to Kevin describing my condition.

Three nights later, I was asleep and then half awoke, feeling hands pressing on the back of my neck and straight away felt something hit my lower spine. My head arched back in a jerk. It's a good thing the hands were there! I knew someone was working on my spine although I couldn't feel anything. I just thought to myself "Well, that's one fusion less" and then went back to sleep.

When I awoke the next morning I couldn't believe I had slept through it all. Normally, if I hear a slight noise, I'm awake and the light is on. Then I found that I could stand up straight from the chair without pain. I couldn't believe it! A week later and I'm still the same.

I wrote to Kevin thanking him. I feel sorry that he's not allowed to cure himself. He really has the power and guides that heal.

Mrs M Shutt, Lancashire

Letter No 10 to Psychic News – September 1999

HEALER KEVIN'S POSTBAG GROWS

Having recently seen so many letters about Kevin McGrath, I feel I must add my words of praise to those already written.

Kevin is a truly remarkable person. If there were a few doubts before reading his wonderful book "Radiant Friends Beside Me" there could be none at all after.

He is very sincere with a simplicity and directness that is both warming and comforting. I had had several occasions when I have phoned either for myself or for friends in need of help and healing and I have each time had good reason to be grateful. The last one was when a very dear member of my family was due to have a very serious throat operation, which proved to be, quite brilliantly, successful. She was quickly up and about after the op and the toast of all the doctors who were bewildered by her speedy recovery.

Indeed there are more things in heaven and earth than any of us can truly understand, though it certainly seems that Kevin holds the key.

Oddly enough though, he is always the first one to direct any praise towards his Guides, and to say that it is they who should take the credit.

I think his modesty is remarkable. Particularly in view of all the praise that has been heaped upon him at various times. I suppose his sympathy comes from his own personal knowledge of pain and suffering and whereas in some it produces bitterness and self-centredness, in him it has the opposite effect. This of course makes him a very willing listener to other people's problems and has strengthened his determination to help when and where he can.

I extend my warmest thanks and good wishes for continued success with all his good work.

Peggy Adams, London N4

Letter No 11 to Psychic News – September 2000

MY THANKS TO KEVIN

I would like, through the pages of Psychic News, to publicly thank Kevin McGrath for the distant healing I have received from him for a very bad back. I had never had such pain.

Immediately I rang him I got great relief. Day by day it has got better and now it feels wonderful. Thank you Kevin McGrath. God bless you.

Jeanette Baggley, Shropshire

Letter No 12 to Psychic News – December 2000

MAN ON A MISSION FOR SPIRITUALISM

J Lester's letter (Psychic News 7th October) was so heart warming that I must tell you how Kevin McGrath totally changed this once hard-nosed and long-standing sceptic into a highly enthusiastic Spiritualist.

In younger days, during my career as a professional cricketer and golfer, I seriously injured my spine and could play no more. I concentrated instead on building a business specialising in sales and teaching within the sporting arena. Fortunately, we are very successful, but, when my back worsened, I was left a near-cripple and somewhat of a passenger to my two business partners.

Over a period of five years, I paid approximately £10,000 to a variety of private medical therapists and finally underwent major private surgery, which was completely unsuccessful and left me in a worse state than before undergoing the knife. Eight weeks ago, by sheer change (or was it?) I rang a kind nursing friend to arrange the return of her "Tens" machine, which also had not worked for me. My friend suggested that I contact medium and healer Kevin McGrath as he had sorted her "incurable" back problem in the late July but she had lost his phone number.

With a glimmer of hope, I attended my local Spiritualist church where a member gave me Kevin McGrath's phone number and advised me to buy the Psychic News from my newsagent; I did so and found it absorbing reading. I rang Kevin and, two weeks later, he treated me with psychic surgery, a concept which I had always regarded as "wacky" but I was now desperate. He informed me that scar tissue caused by the operation was being removed and necessary adjustments were being made to the skeletal structure. The result was simply mind-boggling. My back condition was completely cured after this one treatment – and is still fine to the present time!

My incredible healing experience was obviously engineered to remove my "blinkers" and, needless to say, I have since sent quite a few sceptics to Kevin who have also had their eyes opened, with their various ailments being treated successfully.

I now spend a fair amount of time converting as many folk as possible to the whole world of spiritualism with its profound truths and the priceless services that can be obtained through such highly gifted channels as Kevin McGrath and I would like to extend my deepest thanks to Kevin for being there when I was most needed.

Ronald Haines, Liverpool

CHAPTER FIVE

Psychic Contributions

*Kevin McGrath's natural psychic ability and
inspirational knowledge is clearly highlighted
in the following articles and letter. A random selection of
questions with the appropriate answers on psychic
matters, from a periodic column featured in the
Guardian Newspaper.*

QUESTION AND ANSWER NO 1

Q.   I would like your comments on an extremely frightening psychic occurrence which happened to me recently. I have also heard that some people experience these sensations regularly and wonder what you make of it.

It was 2.35 am when I was awakened by the distinct sensation of feeling very light and appeared to be hovering at ceiling level with a wispy cord from my body, joined to my own sleeping form down on the bed. Worrying that I might not get back, I then returned rapidly to my body. The following morning I tried to convince myself that it had been a dream but I knew it had been very real. The whole experience was very unnerving and I am not sure that I would like it to happen again.

Disturbed, Stockton Heath

A.   Having personally experienced the sensation of "astral projection" on several occasions, I found your out of body account most interesting. This psychic occurrence has been uniformly described by many people from all parts of the globe through the ages.

The human body is comprised of both physical and etheric counterparts. Sometimes, owing to undue stress or possibly a latent psychic development, the spirit body, which is a complete replica of the physical form, can be propelled unexpectedly out of the body, as you clearly describe. This spirit body is always linked to a psychic cord attached to the crown of the head, a location normally known by students of the paranormal as the final "chakra".

I wish to reassure you that whilst experiencing "astral travel" one's guardian spirit angel is in close attendance to ensure that no inferior spirit causes interference endangering a safe return.

QUESTION AND ANSWER No 2

Q. *On my holiday abroad, I went to see a clairvoyant who seemed to be popular. I came away somewhat worried. During the reading, a possible, very serious illness relating to a family member was predicted some time in the future. I have since been much ill at ease. Could she have been wrong? I would appreciate your opinion as it might ease my fears.*

Worried, Newton le Willows

A. The type of clairvoyant reading that you received is by no means uncommon.

My advice is to treat the particular information that caused concern with a large pinch of salt, as it may well have been incorrect.

On a personal note, I would always endeavour, during a reading, to withhold such information received through clairvoyance, from the client, to avoid causing unnecessary distress.

Unfortunately, this form of generalised seership can be experienced within a "passing trade" setting.

In hindsight, you might have been better served consulting a recognised psychic reader closer to home. I feel sure that he or she would have focused properly on your present surrounding cosmic influences and genuinely advised you on future life patterns to suit our individual needs.

QUESTION AND ANSWER No 3

Q. *Please can you tell me your thoughts on reincarnation, as my friends who are strong church goers inform me that it is not true and regard the whole idea as sinful.*

Curious, Warrington

A. Reincarnation, apart from being a compelling doctrine, is no more sinful than Charles Darwin's theory of natural selection. Sadly, the modern church hierarchy does not have an open-minded approach to the growing public interest and wide acceptance of life's inexplicable ups and downs.

Although the mainstream British spiritualist movement has differing ideas on the subject, it is more or less accepted that to evolve properly, the soul must experience the full gamut of its emotions over many lives, each life determined by a lift of the soul's vibrations through free will, until it is evolved and pure enough to escape the heavy pull of the earth's plane.

Communications have frequently been received through mediums from the upper planes of spirit life, which show that the doctrine of reincarnation is a fact.

QUESTION AND ANSWER No 4

Q.   I wonder if you can help me to know if my parents, who died 30 years ago are trying to get in touch with a message through my dreams. I dreamed my later mother and I were walking together when I realised I hadn't bought a birthday card for one of the family.

My mother scolded me for being so concerned and worried, as though the person was not worth it I answered: "That is cruel".

We then approached an empty house. We entered. I chattered away about the improvement I could make to the house. Then I found myself in a downstairs room, completely alone. I left the house to look for my parents.

Outside the house the road was rough and paved with broken paving stones. My father came in sight. He had placed items from a shopping trolley into a zip bag. I asked him "Please don't make the zip bag too heavy". Then I awoke.

I am 76, with bad arthritis. My husband is a very stubborn man. He will not go to see the doctor. I find it exhausting trying to communicate with him as his mind is getting slow and forgetful, relying on me completely. Thank you for Your Problems Shared page.

Bewildered, Warrington

A.   Parents who have been in the spirit world for some considerable time are usually still very much aware of the various problems that face their children who live on the earth plane.

It is quite possible that you may be naturally concerned over family or financial worries and seeking resolutions to the problems presented.

Some of the details that you have mentioned relating to your dreams are probably due to the subconscious mind, symbolically unravelling the relevant unresolved anxieties.

However, I am of the opinion that your parents are communicating to you within your dream state. The message conveyed should be construed as an assurance that they are providing strong spiritual support to help you through any difficulties which you may be experiencing.

QUESTION AND ANSWER NO 5

Q.   *My friend and I are considering using a ouija board to contact certain deceased persons, but I remembered that in an article some years ago, you warned people against using them for spirit communications, as there were serious dangers involved. Would you please explain fuller about this.*

Curious, Warrington

A.   My previous viewpoint on the dangerous usage of the ouija board has not changed. I have encountered various evil and hostile spirit entities over the years, necessitating very strong exorcism, all presenting considerable resistance. A good percentage had initially been openly invited by well meaning but naïve folk carelessly using the ouija board in a home setting.

Your desire to make communication with the spirit world in this uncontrolled manner may send an immediate signal to the discarnate groups of "riff-raff" which frequently congregate in the corridors of the astral plane which is adjacent to our own earth plane. If given the chance, these inferior and troublesome souls would quickly grasp the opportunity to wreak psychic havoc on the unfortunate contacts.

If, for bona-fide reasons, you and your friends still intend to seek contact with souls who have passed on, I would recommend a consultation with a reputable spiritual medium or alternatively, attend a service within a Spiritualist National Union affiliated church. Both options will offer realistic safeguards for your future mental and physical well being.

QUESTION AND ANSWER No 6

Q.   *I believe that I am dying and that there is somewhere else that we eventually go to. Nonetheless I worry that when my life ends, that I will not be at peace, and receive much punishment on the other side for my wrong doings during my life. Could you allay my fears and enlighten me on this subject.*

Fearful, Woolston

A.   According to communications received via higher spirit intelligentsia, God has a merciful and very fair system which deals with sinful souls.

Without exception, all human beings commit sin, both great and small. Generally, the messages conveyed, unless one chooses to remain earthbound state that, on the death of the physical body, the soul's transition is carefully arranged through a process strictly in line with natural law.

At the moment of physical death, one is not automatically lifted up to paradise or despatched into a state of purgatorial limbo, or worse still, hurled into the fiery depths of hell.

Instead, a gentle welcome awaits the soul from angelic guides within a restful spirit realm, where associated loves ones, including pets, patiently wait to greet the newly arrived soul.

A period of honest and enlightening self-reflection of the earth life that has been experienced will follow, with a subsequent amicable acceptance of the resultant placement in a spirit realm, high or low, appropriately matching soul vibration.

In reality, the main interpretation of the higher spirit messages received concerning God's law of spirit evolution, determines that each soul on physical death, will always eventually gravitate to a spirit plane of consciousness where it will join other discarnate individuals of a similar disposition and rate of soul growth.

Spiritual healing has now also been requested to help ease your serious health situation.

QUESTION AND ANSWER NO 7

Q.   *I am a charge nurse in an elderly care home in Warrington. We appear to be experiencing unexplained noises. Also, occasionally, individuals, old and very young appear then disappear.*

Up to now they appear harmless. The staff are a little wary and nervous.

What could be the cause and is there anything that I can do myself to understand these experiences? Is there anything I can do of a practical nature?

A.   The unexplained noises that you and your staff have experienced are most likely to be caused by earthbound spirits that have also periodically materialised as described.

Because of the intermittent periods of souls passing on from their physical lives in your place of employment, residual fields of psychic energy are formed which allow spirits to manifest more easily.

The paranormal haunting activity is probably a signal that release from their earthbound state is being requested.

As you have indicated that you are prepared to help the lost and confused souls to find their way to their rightful spirit realms, I have sent you a gentle soul rescue procedure which is appropriate for the task in hand.

If you are apprehensive about carrying out the prayer service as suggested, please let me know, as I shall be pleased to carry out the necessary procedures for you.

QUESTION AND ANSWER No 8

Q. I *have enjoyed your forthright answers and warmth to people who have written to you. I write asking you to help me with two issues of an eerie nature and would appreciate your views.*

When I go on holiday, either abroad or at home, I seem to instantly recognise locations and buildings I have never visited before. Sometimes I know what can be found round corners and I am always very accurate.

The other problem is that, when I am in the company of other people who are suffering with illnesses, although they have not told me the exact problem, I always pick up the symptoms. The pain and unease is with me for some time, and disturbs me quite a lot.

A.   It would appear that you are naturally sensitive to the spirit dimensions.

Your clear knowledge of places and buildings that you have not previously visits is an obvious case of what is known as "déjà vu". In paranormal terms, there is a very strong chance that you have lived a past life in the locations visited.

The ability to experience other people's painful symptoms in such a precise manner shows that you possess an obvious psychic gift associated with the power of spiritual healing.

Should you wish to further develop your psychic gifts, and spiritual gifts, the Spiritualist National Union Church network operates classes that safely help you to realise your full potential in that regard.

LETTER TO PSYCHIC NEWS – JULY 1996

CAN WE HAVE PSYCHIC PREDICTIONS IN PN?

I have read with interest the recent articles in Psychic News highlighting the differences between psychics and mediums and it seems that some are equally gifted in each discipline.

You have featured letters from a number of people (including myself) who have greatly benefited from the healing works of Kevin McGrath and his guides and you will know that Kevin is equally regarded for his most impressive record of soul rescue and other psychic works.

He certainly earned his credentials as a psychic with the accuracy (unfortunately) of his prediction of the recent massive Californian earthquake that was outlined in the February issue of **Maxim**, a high-volume international magazine and I'm sure that he'd have more to offer if approached.

I wonder, would it be possible for other well-known psychics, who have contributed to PN, to provide readers with their own predictions for the post-millennium age?

Terry Hands, Northampton

CHAPTER SIX

Concluding Sequence

The final sequence of this true, documented book is a typical and very spooky factual haunting episode that occurred in 1996, recently written by Kevin McGrath for publication. I would also wish to point out to the reader, that the many paranormal case histories and psychic conversations within the book's chapters are only the tip of the iceberg, considering the huge volume of spiritual services that Kevin has rendered "behind the scenes" to his fellow souls, both in the UK and overseas over the period covered by the published articles. In light of the overwhelming evidential material that has been covered, may he keep well and strong to continue with his genuine, selfless and unique psychic work, that has benefited so many people in need.

My simple tribute to him is the writing of this book.

HOUSE OF FEAR – January 2002

Factual Account of a double haunting

On a wet and windy evening during the month of October 1996, arriving back home to the town of Warrington, Cheshire, from a most rewarding psychic – forum that I had provided in Rossendale, Lancashire. I decided to leave the milk order near the rear gate before retiring to bed. As the bottles were placed in their box, on returning, I brushed against the remnants of our treasured honeysuckle bush. It had truly repaid me with a profusion of glorious, scented flowers, following my removal of its carpet of unwelcome black-fly visitors, which threatened its very life.

It was not long before I was to be involved in a most interesting, but daunting, spiritual battle. For, during the next two months, I was to be confronted with another formidable task of fighting and overcoming pure evil. However, on the lighter side through a soul rescue, part of my duty would also bring great satisfaction. The experience would also reinforce many hard-held opinions amongst the psychic fraternity, that Warrington, with a history dating from 90 AD, is indeed one of the most ghost-infested towns in the United Kingdom.

Within my neighbourhood, close to the main town Cemetery, off Manchester Road, a large empty, grimy and white painted four bedroomed house was situated. This was chiefly noticeable because of the frequent appearances of "For Sale" signs that swung from its front door frame.

Over a period of thirty years I discovered, from long-established neighbours, that no fewer than ten families had moved out after brief spells of residence, all complaining of unbearable haunting activity. Their eerie accounts told to neighbours were neither misplaced nor flights of fancy imaginations, as I had already experienced a quite serious psychic episode of phenomena, whilst passing the dwelling, twelve months earlier.

During the previous year, in early October, I decided to visit a friend who lived close to the house. As I approached the front elevation, its malevolence chilled me to the bone. A powerful evil atmosphere was being absorbed by my whole being. On moving past the side entrance door, which was partly glazed, the interior light was unaccountably switched on and instantaneously, the ugliest of male spirit faces rammed itself against the glass pane, in an obvious attempt to cause intimidation. Knowing of its owner's inferior persona, humour proved to be the ideal riposte, so I responded with a wry smile, clairvoyantly communicating to him that I had taken his gesture and presence on board for future attention. He quickly disappeared and the house fell back again into complete darkness.

I instinctively knew that at some future time, I would be engaged in a significant and forceful struggle with the ungodly spirit entity, that I had unexpectedly encountered.

The following weekend, I made a visit to a popular confectionery shop in the Town Centre to purchase some lozenges. Whilst being served by the elderly lady owner,

I recalled that she and her family had spent a brief period in the haunted house.

Being a trifle curious, I asked her why she had moved out so quickly. Knowing of my psychic leanings, she informed me of an unnerving, paranormal experience that during one evening, whilst her family were watching the television in the living room, she decided to wash the dishes and clean up the kitchen. As she emptied the sink bowl, several lines of writing suddenly appeared on the doors of the cupboard units, the contents being of a lewd and menacing nature.

They were visible for several minutes, her desperate calls to her husband and daughter to witness their appearance went unheeded, and when they finally popped into the kitchen, the writing had vanished. From that moment, no amount of persuasion could change her mind that moving house was a priority. She sold cheaply and moved four months later.

I thanked her for her time and left, nursing an increased determination to carry out whatever was required, when the higher side decided it was the appropriate time to resolve the whole unpleasant haunting problem.

Three weeks later, in the final days of October, during a moonlit, Thursday evening, I felt impelled to take some old sporting magazines to a pal who collected them as a hobby. I knew that there was a distinct possibility that he could be found imbibing his favourite guest beer in a nearby traditional pub. I left my home with the magazines tucked under my arm.

My journey was on the route where the haunted house, previously mentioned, was located. It did strike an uncomfortable chord in my thoughts that the night had a soul-jolting surprise in store for me.

Ten minutes later I approached the large white house which was gaining such a frightening reputation and crossed the road to take a short cut along the adjacent back of the next street. The dwelling was still dark, empty and each window had its blinds fully drawn.

My apprehensive demeanour was immediately kick-started, as the blinds of the side living room were abruptly parted. The light of the moon beamed onto the clear spirit figure of an old woman dressed in a cardigan and skirt, whose face was filled with sheer horror. She was staring directly at me, shrieking loudly and hammering on the glass pane although an opening light, which could easily have been opened, was fixed above on the window frame. I had to come to terms with the fact that this lady was possibly in spirit form and her mindset was closed to a state of incarceration. She continued to scream in an incoherent manner. My ears began to buzz at a very high pitch, verifying that it was indeed a materialisation of a very desperate female spirit entity, seeking help. She was undoubtedly suffering unspeakable abuse from the evil spirit that I had previously encountered. In the space of five minutes I had experienced a wide range of psychic senses - physical mediumship, clairvoyance, clairsentience and clairaudience, which did help me to assess the intriguing, unearthly factors of the situation.

I stepped towards the window and communicated to the imprisoned spirit that it was impossible for me to gain access at that moment but, promised that I would return and somehow enter this property to effect her release. For good measure I conveyed my intentions to the evil male spirit that he was now top of my list for future exorcism.

Taking a few deep breaths, I continued on my way to the pub still marvelling at the incredible manner in which the distressed earthbound lady spirit had bided her time, waited for my precise journey that night and managed, God only knows how, to summon a vast surge of psychic power, enough to enable her to attract my attention in such mind-boggling fashion.

Instinct told me that my spirit helpers had surely intervened to provide her with the psychic strength that she truly was in great need of, to be lifted out of her appalling earthbound state.

Confirming that the whole experience was not a delusion, which is possible, for I had never previously experienced a spirit manifestation in such external circumstances, apart from my earlier unforgettable meeting with an angel on a public bench, who had materialised in order to test my charitable credentials. As I continued walking, albeit slowly, still absorbing the event and possible future options, my spirit guides quietly conveyed to me that before I entered the pub – a fox would appear to me, standing in the midst of a small grassed cemetery clearing – look at me and then, walk away into the surrounding shrubs.

My spirit helpers were once again incredibly accurate for the fox did indeed greet me, as predicted, and then moved off into the night. I strode into the pub, knowing that a very strong soul rescue and exorcism was looming ever closer and deep into my psyche, I increasingly welcomed the opportunity to be utilised.

I certainly felt that my psychic batteries were being charged up. Paying a visit to my Building Society branch to draw out some cash and check out a sort code, this confirmation was swiftly introduced. The Branch had recently been completely refurbished and as I shuffled my way up the queue, I found myself standing under a large "state of the art" clock. It immediately stopped! The Manager glanced rather curiously at me and remarked – "Mr McGrath, I think it would have been more beneficial if you had used the external cash dispenser and allowed us all to enjoy the clock for a few days at least!" I took the banter in good heart and replied "Sorry – it's not my fault that I am an alien!"

A similar incident happened that night in my local pub. When ordering a drink, standing in line with the electronic till, the barmaid remonstrated with me as it, too, had stopped functioning. I again proffered my apologies.

The next night, before popping off to sleep, to satisfy my curiosity and possible preparation, I meditated and linked up with my spirit guides in order to establish the background of the two earthbound spirits that haunted the previously mentioned large white house.

Information was provided that both spirit entities had lived and died in the dwelling at different periods in the middle part of the century. The lady, a gentle person, had lived alone and was regarded as a recluse. On leaving her physical body, she remained convinced that she had not 'died' and continued to exist in a lonely and confused state, refusing all attempts by angelic helpers to escort her through to the spirit realms.

The male spirit had been throughout his life a callous and cruel individual who had treated his wife and children badly, with both physical and mental abuse, eventually forcing them to leave him after several years of misery, obviously for their safety. His behaviour had become increasingly more violent. He too remained alone in the house and on his death and, with his fervent wish to remain earthbound, the subsequent hell he inflicted upon the lady in spirit, finally convinced her that she was indeed trapped on the earth plane and that she had experienced physical death.

A varied week of psychic readings, sittings and spiritual healing provided me with a vital breathing space and a pleasant distraction from my unfinished spirit clearance task that permeated my daily thoughts.

On the following Monday I decided to visit the estate agents in an attempt to gain access to the house. They were selling the property for an engineer, who worked overseas for an oil company and unfortunately for him, he had bought the house as an investment to sell on for profit but he had never taken up residence.

Arriving at the office I briefly informed them of my plans. The staff quickly made it very clear that prospective purchasers were not being informed of the growing haunting allegations and the vendor would strongly reinforce their viewpoint. The house sale was paramount, whatever the cost in future problems that would be presented to the buyer. I was ushered out with uncomfortable haste. Somewhat frustrated, I returned home and sat quietly in my front room figuring out possible ways of gaining access to the property. My thought patterns were quickly interrupted with the reassuring voice of "Brother Paul", my guardian spirit, a Franciscan monk, a truly advanced soul, whose final earth incarnation had taken place three hundred years ago. "Please relax, it will shortly be arranged for you to accomplish the necessary task which we know is long overdue for Godly intervention. Before you leave the house at any future time, please take with you your rosary set and holy water container for unexpected usage. God Bless!"

Two weeks later, well insulated with the thickest of woollen sweaters, for the weather had become quite cold, I took some clothing and books to the Oxfam charity shop in the Town Centre, met a few friends, enjoyed the saucy "chin-wags" and returned home. Whilst approaching the problematic house which was on my route, my feelings of pessimism were swiftly overturned. A car had stopped outside the side entrance of the dwelling and the young male driver stepped out and opened the door. I quickly concluded that it was the vendor, obviously on holiday and taking the opportunity to check the services, etc and collect his mail. My rosary and crucifix were promptly placed around my neck, a protective prayer said, and the holy water bottle was readied. He was so immersed in reading his mail that when I knocked upon the door, which was half-open, it flashed through my mind that this was the time for action. Politely asking him if I could view the house, he muttered "Sorry but you will have to be quick, once I have checked the meters and read my mail, I will be away. But if you fancy it, get your offer in as it is a bargain!" The fact that it had been on the market for eighteen months had conveniently slipped his memory.

Taking full advantage of his permission, I hurriedly moved into the front living room where I saw the vivid spirit figure of the poor lady, who had previously beckoned me so desperately for assistance. She was cowering in the corner and, on seeing me, straightened up, displaying great relief.

I reassured her that she would soon be at peace and then automatically carried out a full procedure of prayer and soul rescue, blessing the room simultaneously. She began to smile and was instantly showered with the most beautiful colours of gold and purple. Her guardian angel – who had waited so long for her co-operation – stepped forward and gently escorted her upwards on a glorious beam of light, taking her to the summerlands of the spirit world.

The soul rescue had taken five minutes and to utilise precious time that was left, I was anxious to "lock horns" with the evil spirit who I knew was lurking upstairs in the rear bedroom and effect his permanent removal. I suspected that, on completion of the exorcism, he would gravitate to one of the lower hell planes but accepted that the placement would fall in line with universal laws to complement his low spirit vibrations.

The vendor was still sifting through his mail oblivious to my presence. I politely manoeuvred around him to climb up the stairs. As I entered the rear bedroom, a metal ashtray was instantly hurled at me, fortunately missed me and crashed against the door architrave. A freezing cold blast of air also directed at me, momentarily shook my consciousness. Rapidly gathering my purpose and will, I then focused on a huge, shabby and darkly clad male spirit entity; his features were diabolically ugly with large staring eyes that clearly reflected a hatred of my presence. Our paths had definitely crossed before, the previous year. He began voicing all manner of threats and the unholiest of obscenities. Being aware, he knew of my long-held intentions and was not prepared to leave without a struggle. An obnoxious smell of body odour did not help matters. No doubt reflecting his total lack of personal hygiene when in the physical body and obviously still feeling comfortable with the unpleasant smell, he moved towards me. A clumsy lunge towards my neck was made in an attempt to break away my crucifix. Much to my surprise his power caused me to stumble sideways, but the exorcism was uppermost in my mind and I quickly commenced the invocation of the Christ-force with all the powerful prayers that were needed to effect his transition.

The exorcism was repeated three times to intensify its effectiveness, as the evil spirit's power had to be totally depleted. Time was running out fast and I admit to uncomfortable feelings of anxiousness over the vendor pressuring me to leave.

Understandably, I was elated when I finally saw the spirit entity being propelled through the astral barriers, for him to be placed in his rightful realm in the spirit world. His departure was accompanied by a tremendous expulsion of power, which reverberated throughout the room.

My promise to the gentle, but tormented earthbound spirit lady had been kept and with the clearance of this evil male spirit, peace and serenity would now prevail at the house.

I slowly descended down the stairway, passing the vendor with a smile, who had finished with his duties and was waiting for my impressions of the dwelling. He mischievously asked "Did you fall over, there was a bit of a noise?" I told him that I had accidentally dropped an ashtray. Truthfully it had nearly dissected my head, when it had been maliciously and unsuccessfully thrown at me by the departed evil entity!

I thanked him, but was honest enough to admit that the dwelling was unsuitable, four bedrooms would be superfluous to my requirements. Although slightly disappointed he accepted my explanations.

That evening, I spent almost two hours resting on the front room floor, as I truly felt exhausted from my spiritual efforts.

A nice glass of brandy was taken before I retired to bed as my own spirits were in dire need of upliftment. The whole disturbing episode, spanning a period of fifteen months, had indeed left an indelible mark on my soul.